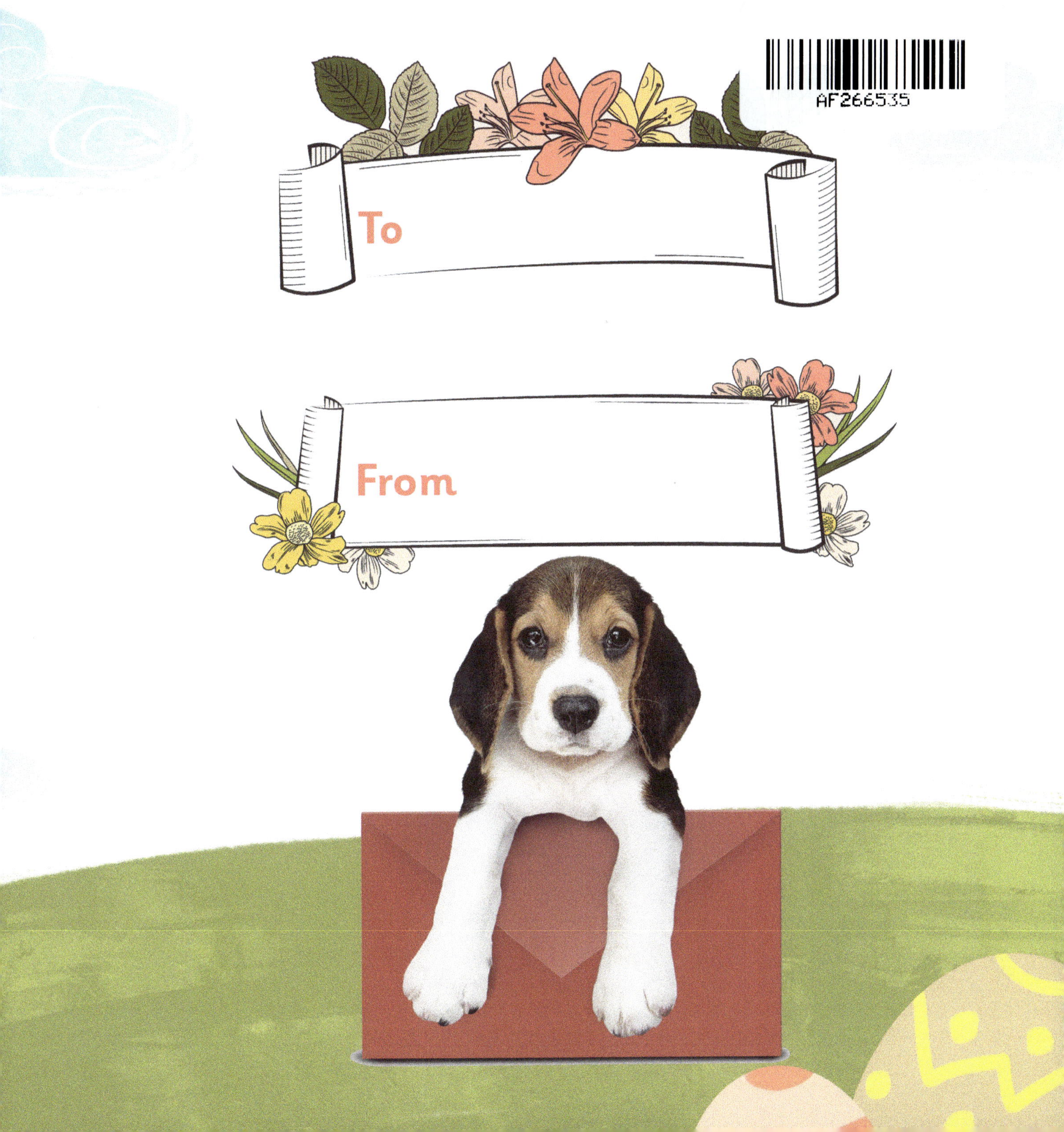

To
From
AF266535

From the moment you were born,
your grandma fell in love with you,
and she will always be there to
offer you her unconditional love
and support.

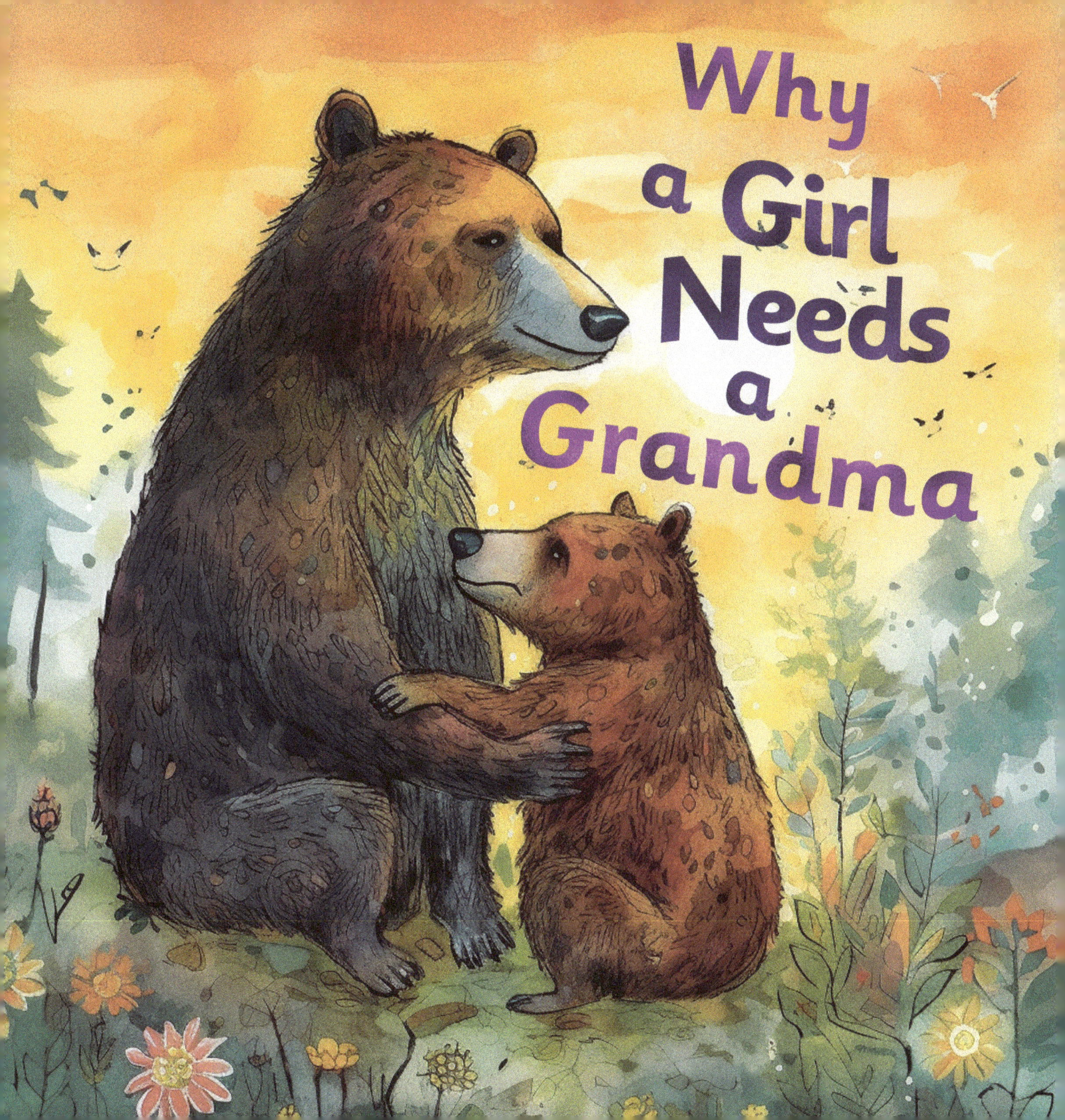

Why
a Girl
Needs
a
Grandma

Get Free Coloring Book send a Mail After Purchase to
jonathanHillBooks@gmail.com

Dedicated to my sons, *Videl, Vishal & Valen*

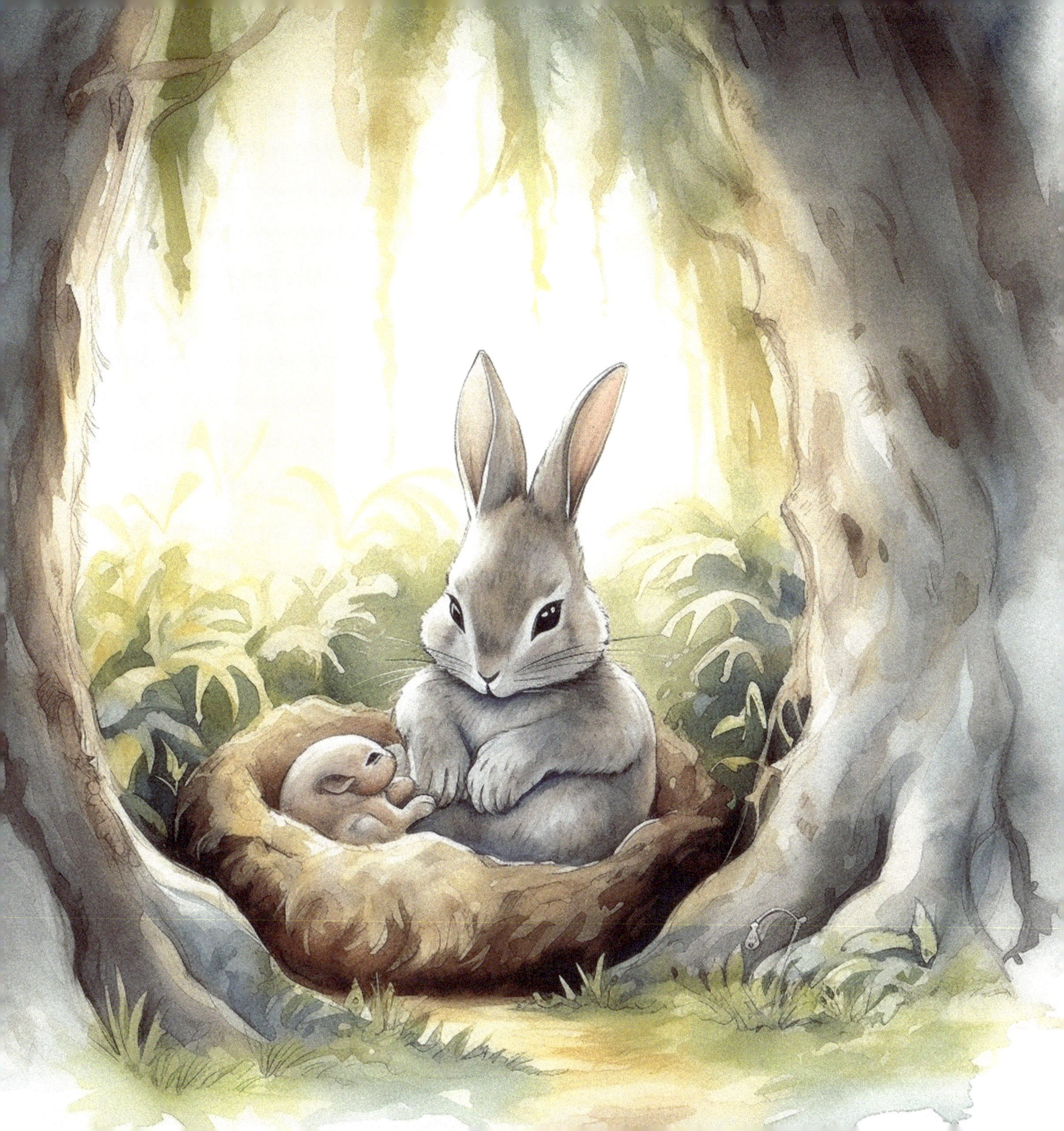

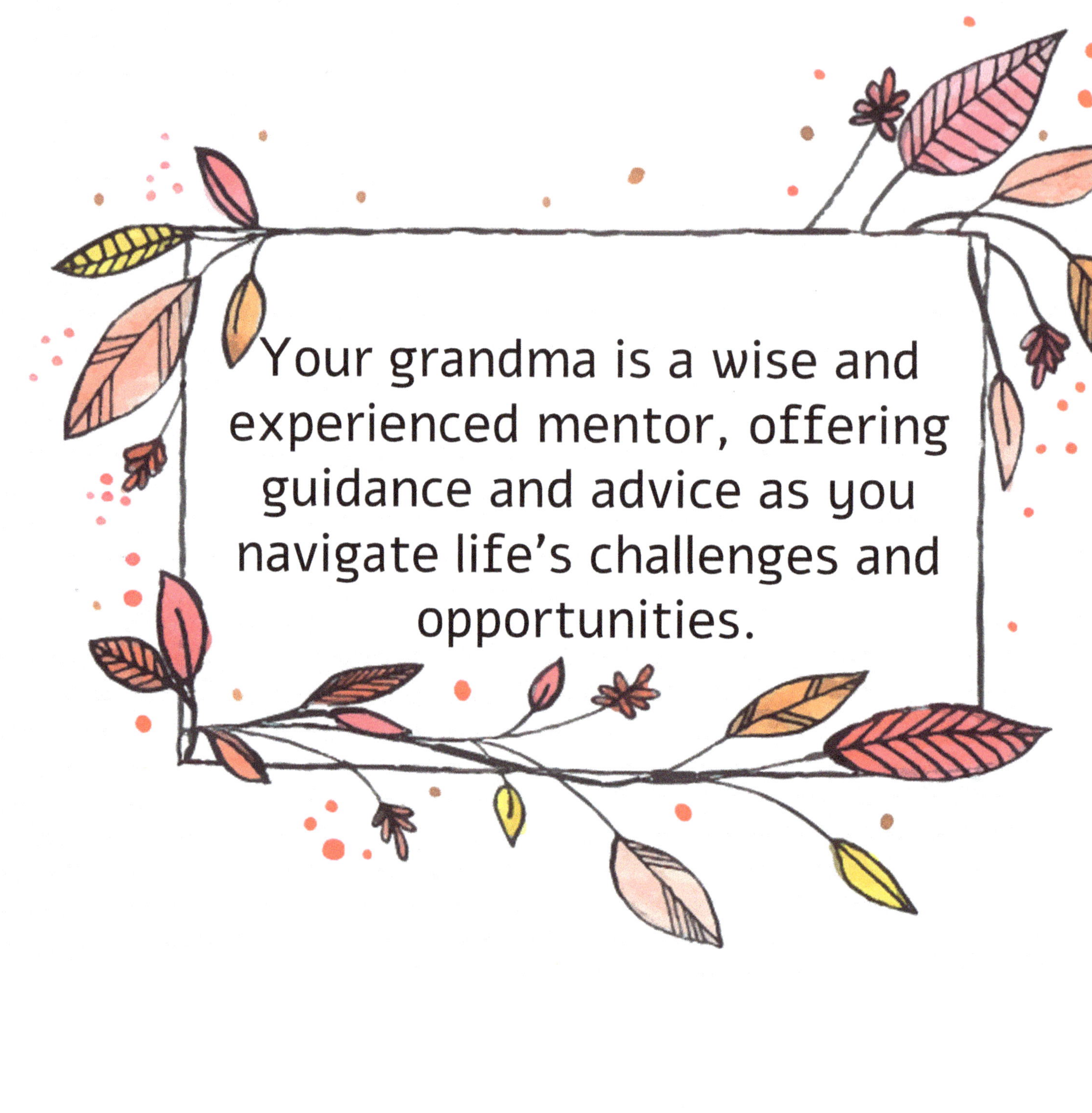

Your grandma is a wise and experienced mentor, offering guidance and advice as you navigate life's challenges and opportunities.

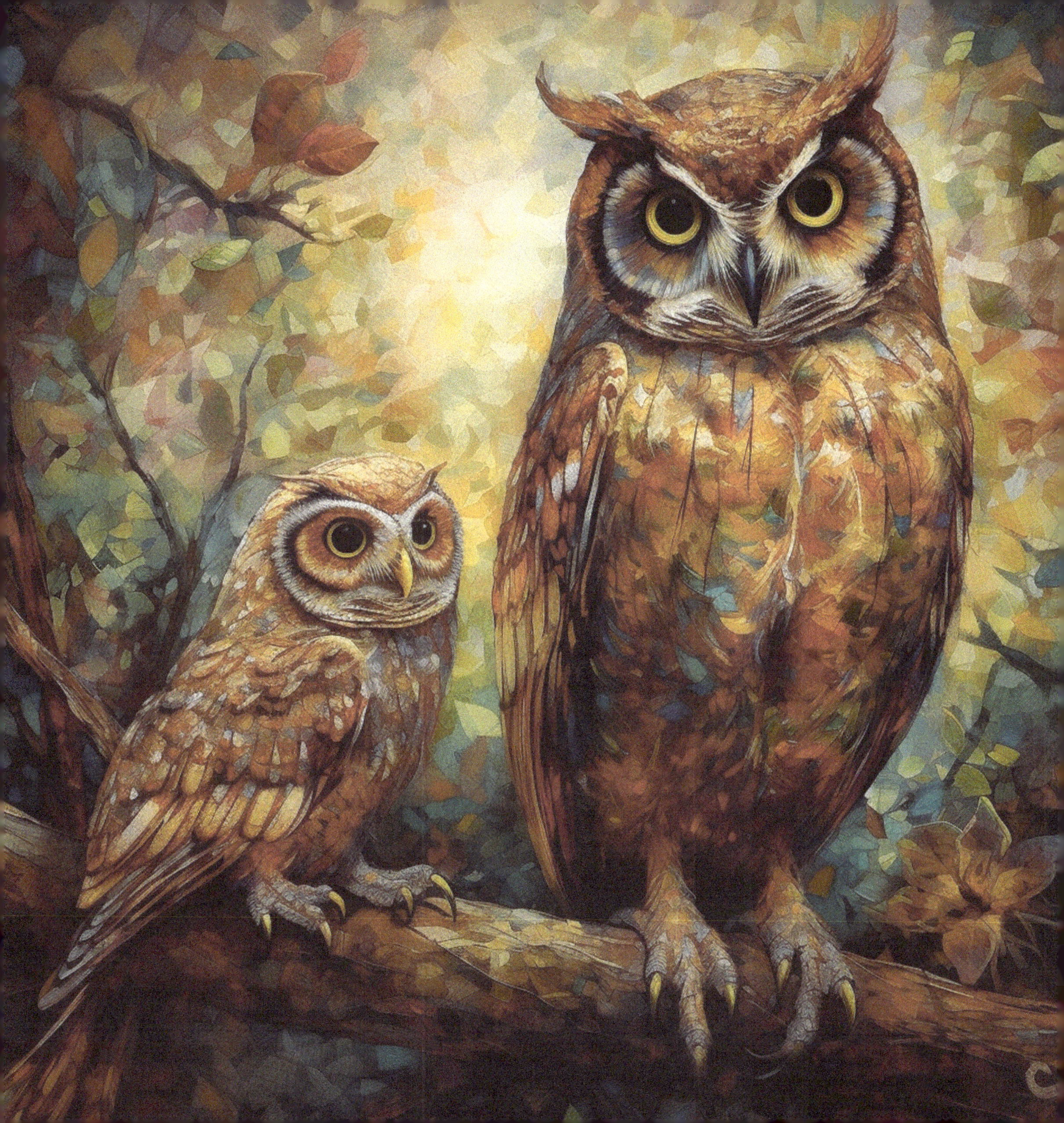

With her warm hugs and kind smile, your grandma is a beacon of love and light in your life, always reminding you of your worth and your potential.

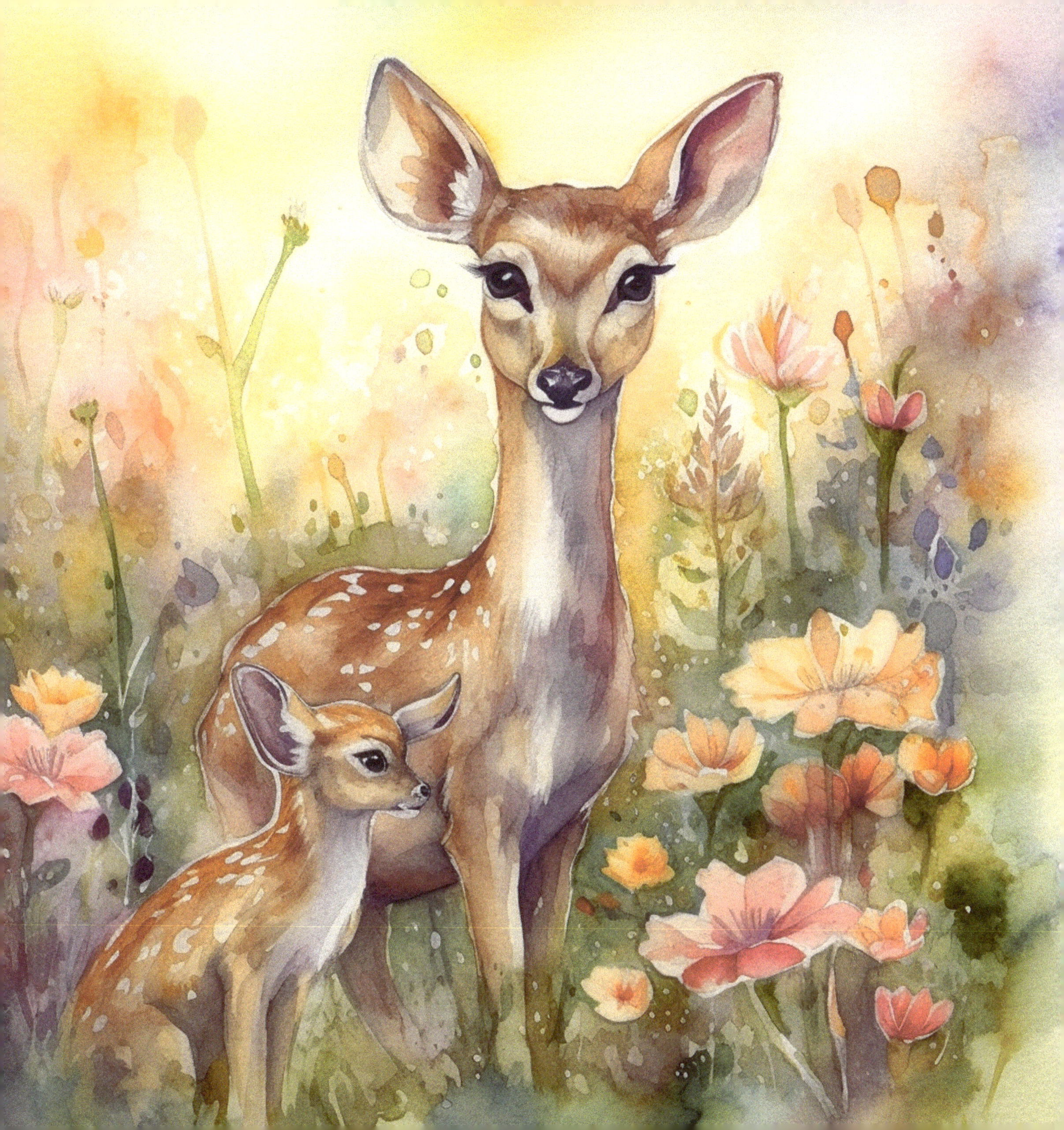

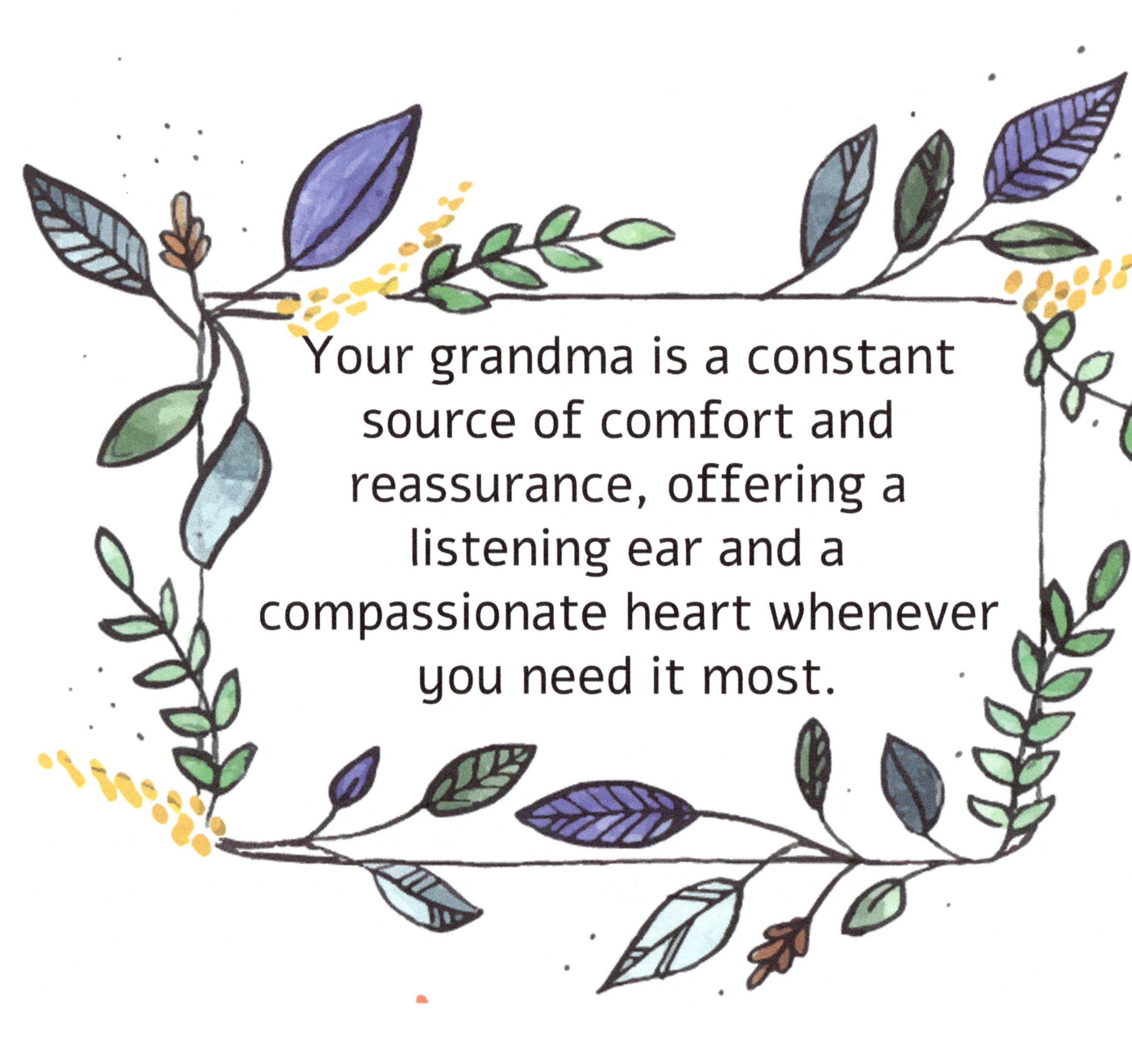
Your grandma is a constant
source of comfort and
reassurance, offering a
listening ear and a
compassionate heart whenever
you need it most.

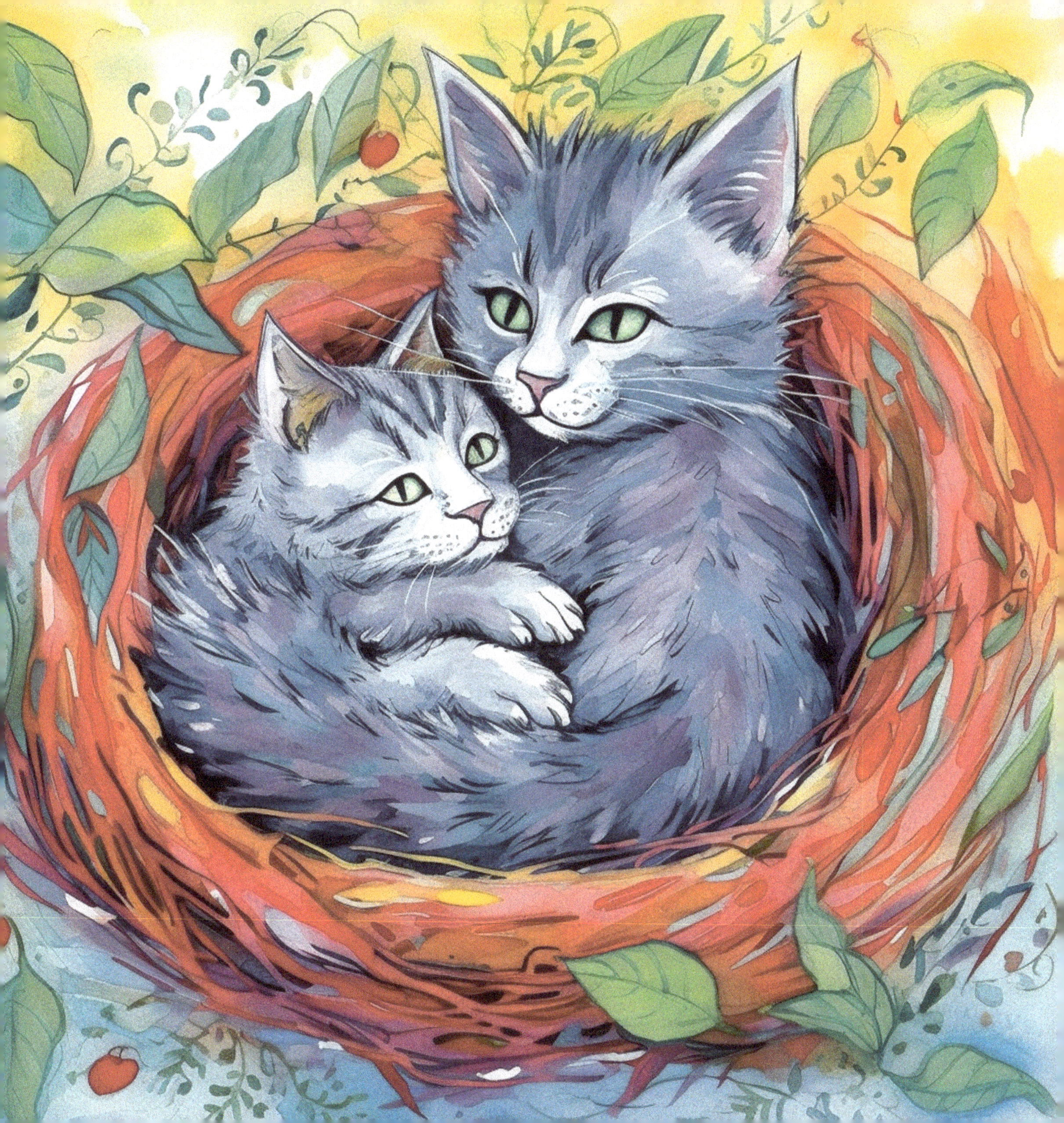

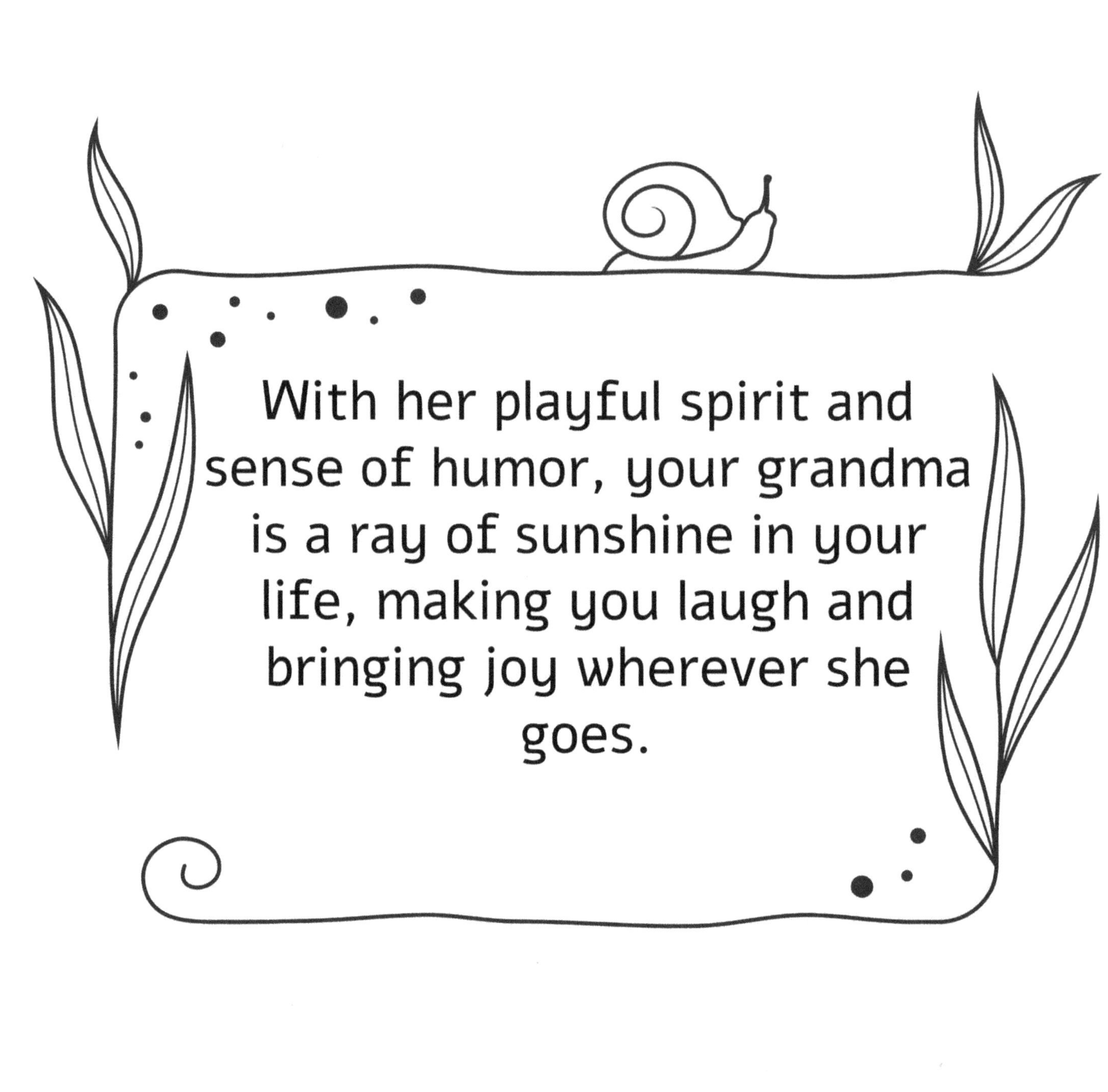

With her playful spirit and sense of humor, your grandma is a ray of sunshine in your life, making you laugh and bringing joy wherever she goes.

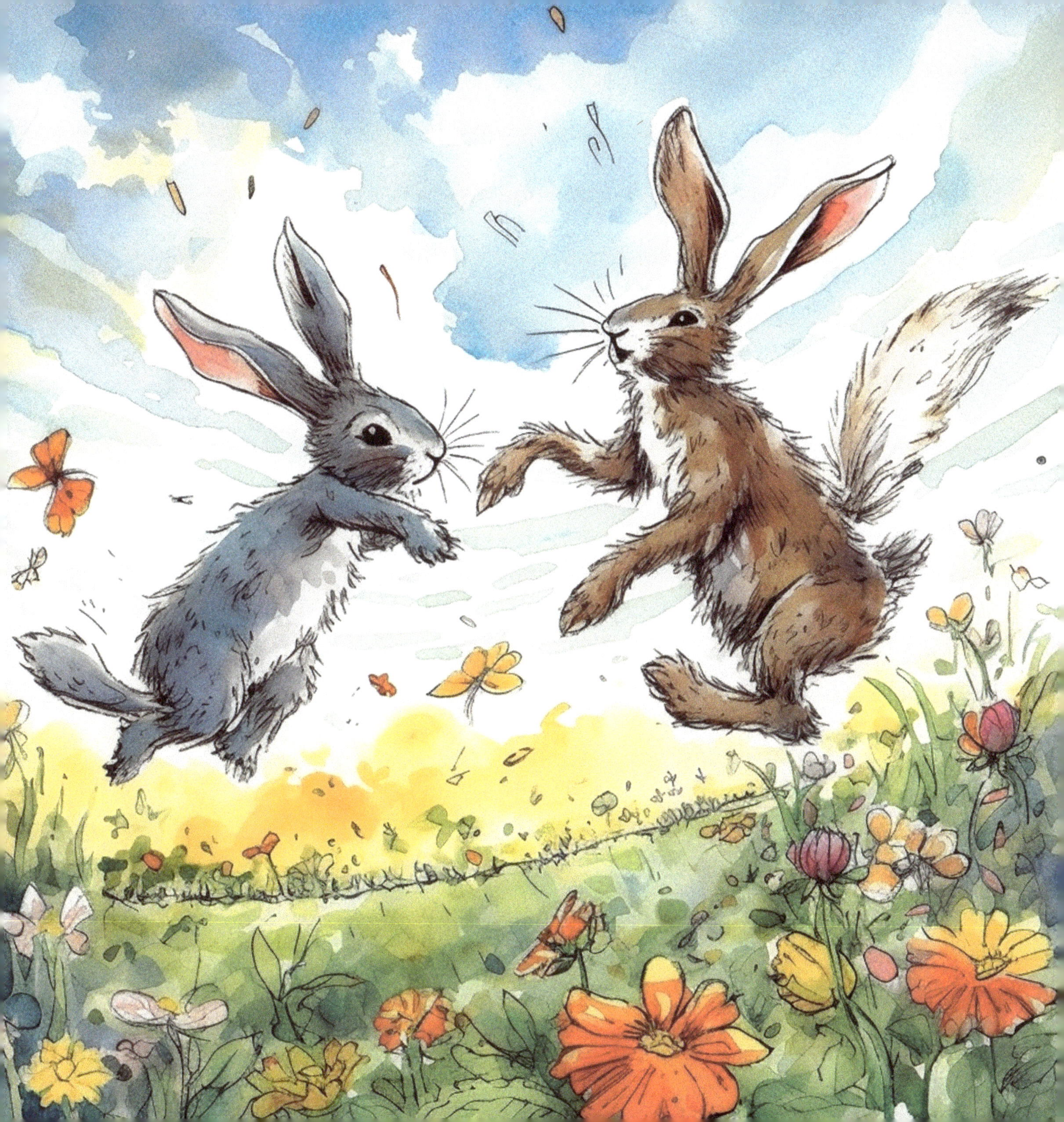

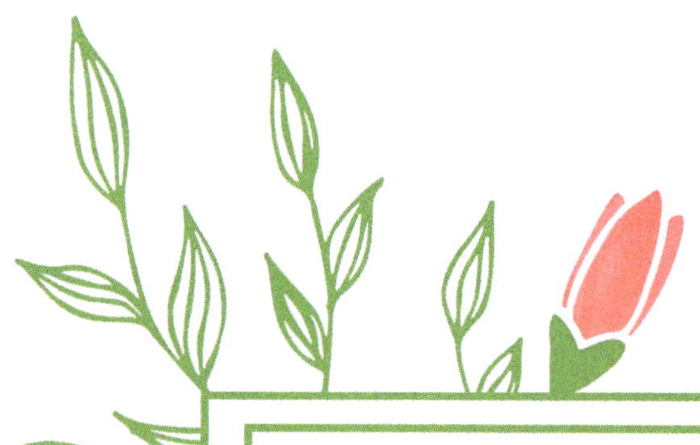

Your grandma is the ultimate role model of grace and resilience, showing you how to weather life's storms with strength and dignity.

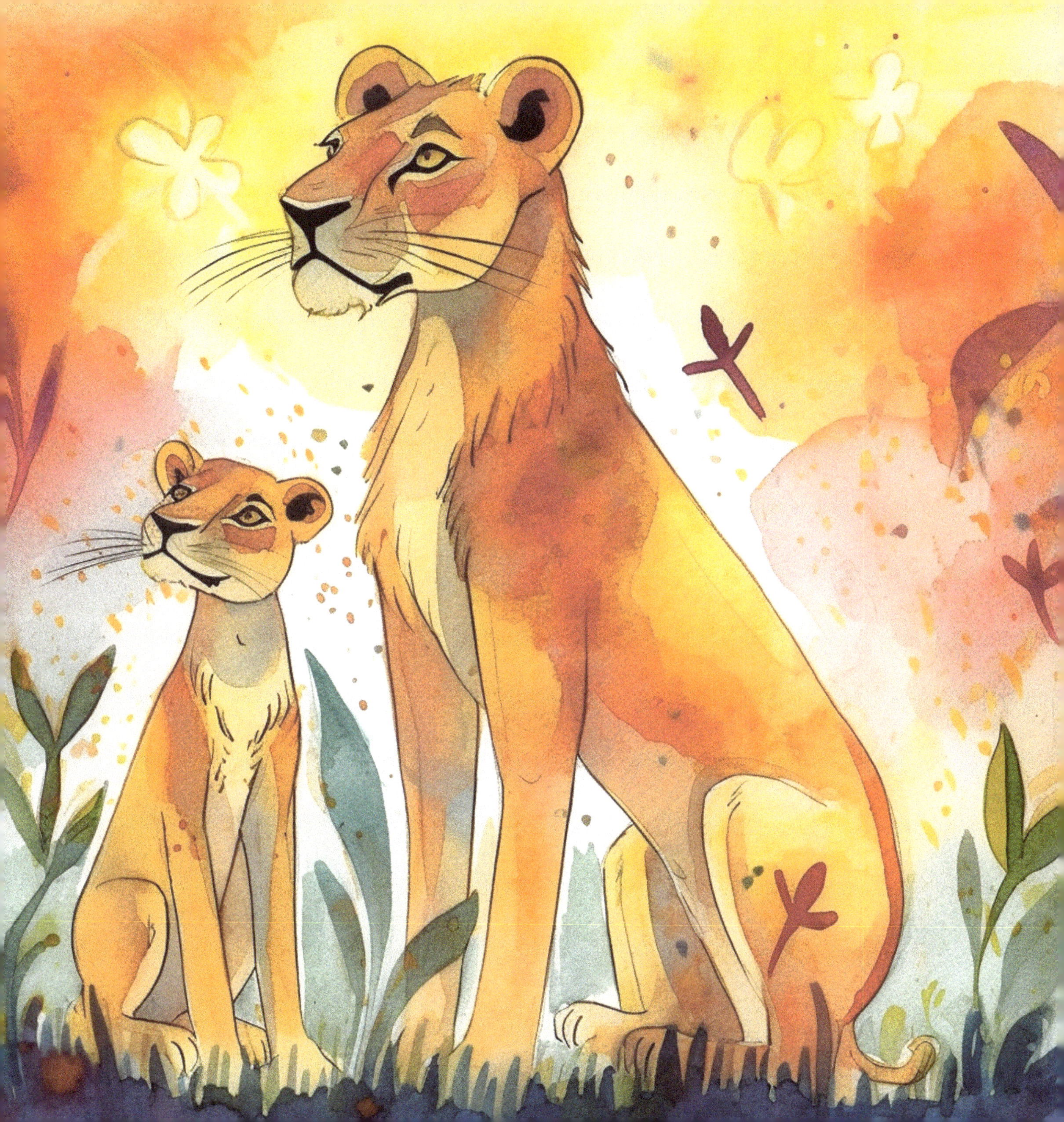

With her gentle guidance and
unwavering support, your
grandma helps you become
the best version of yourself,
inspiring you to reach for your
dreams and live your best life.

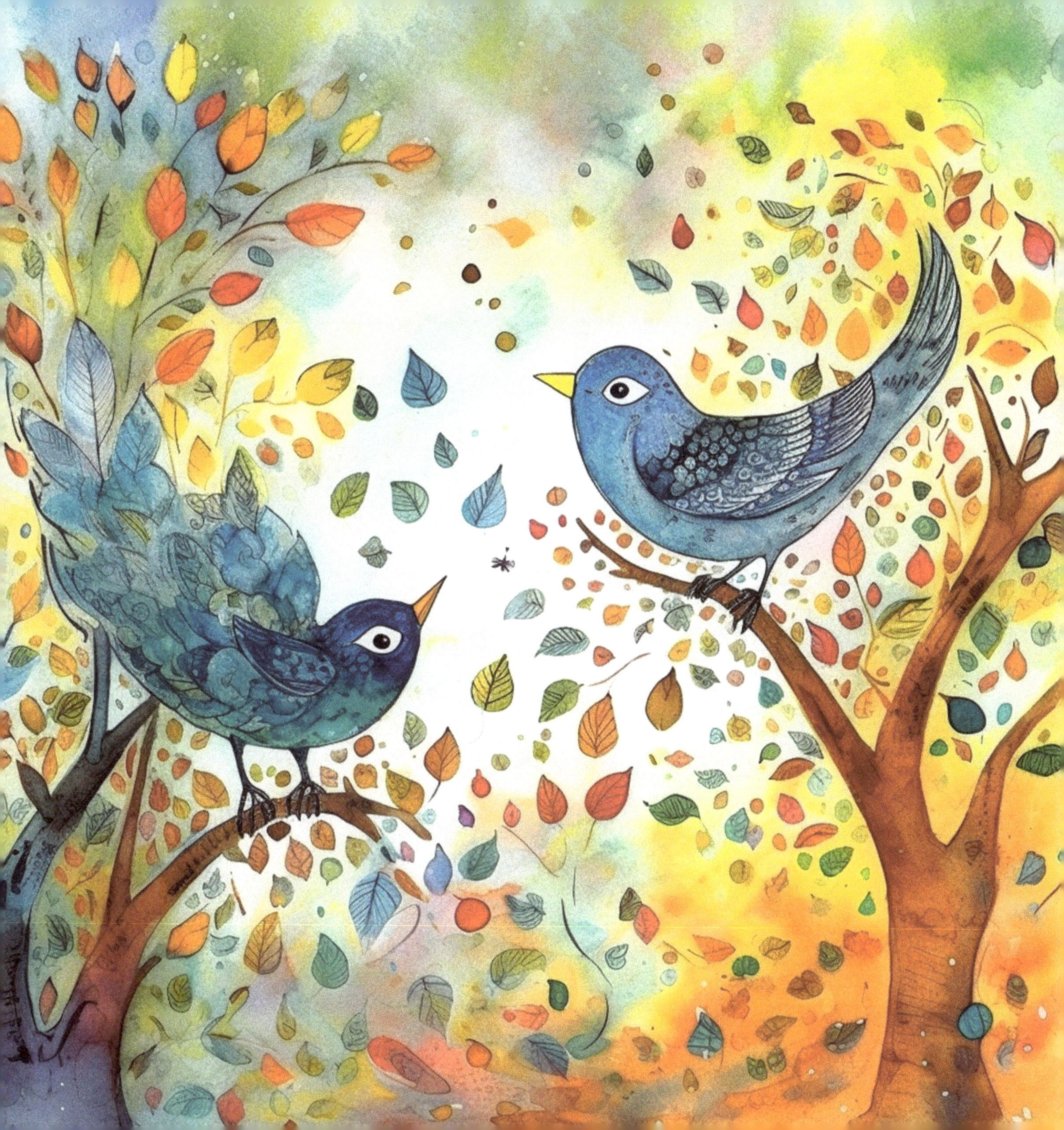

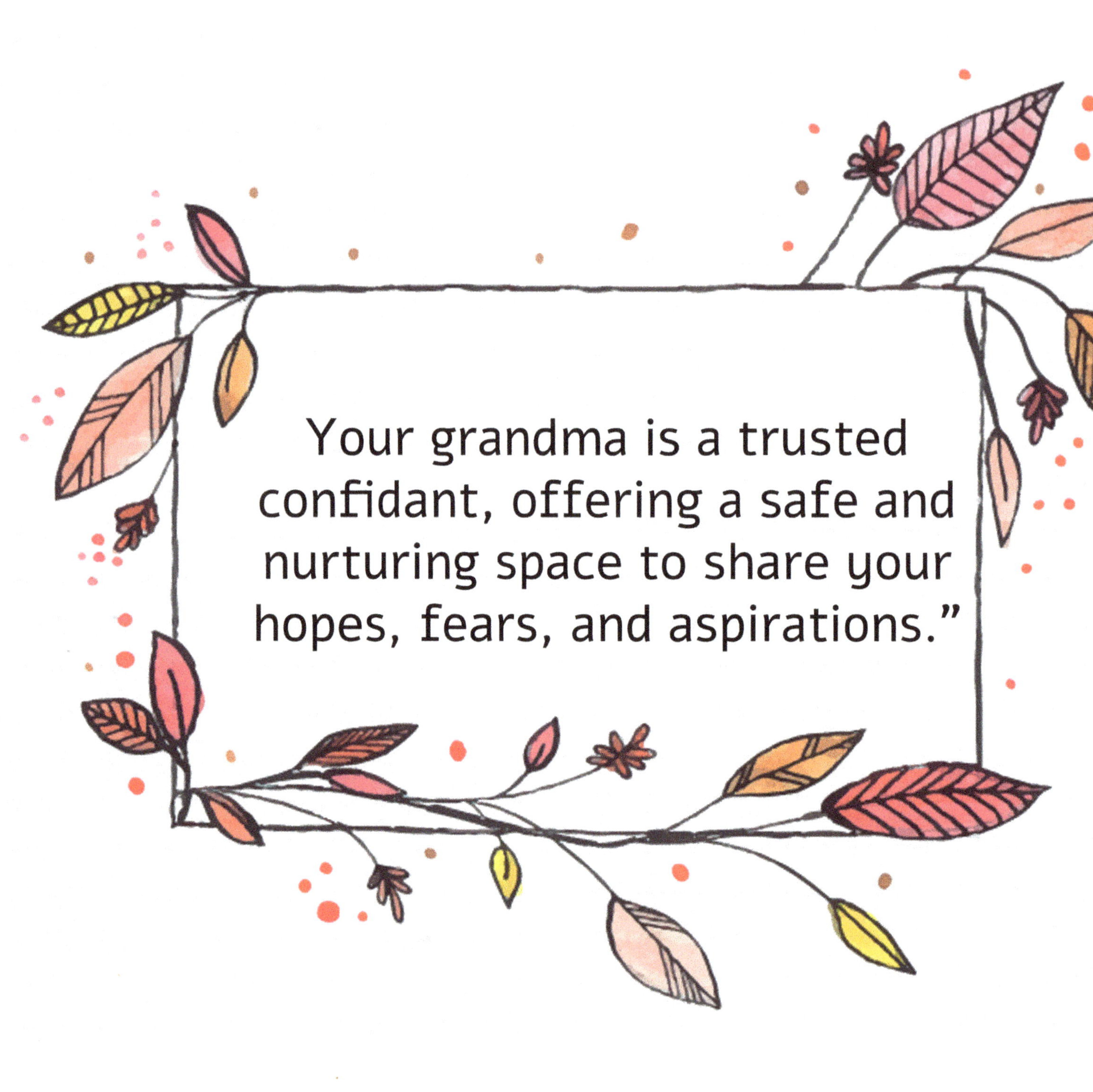

Your grandma is a trusted confidant, offering a safe and nurturing space to share your hopes, fears, and aspirations."

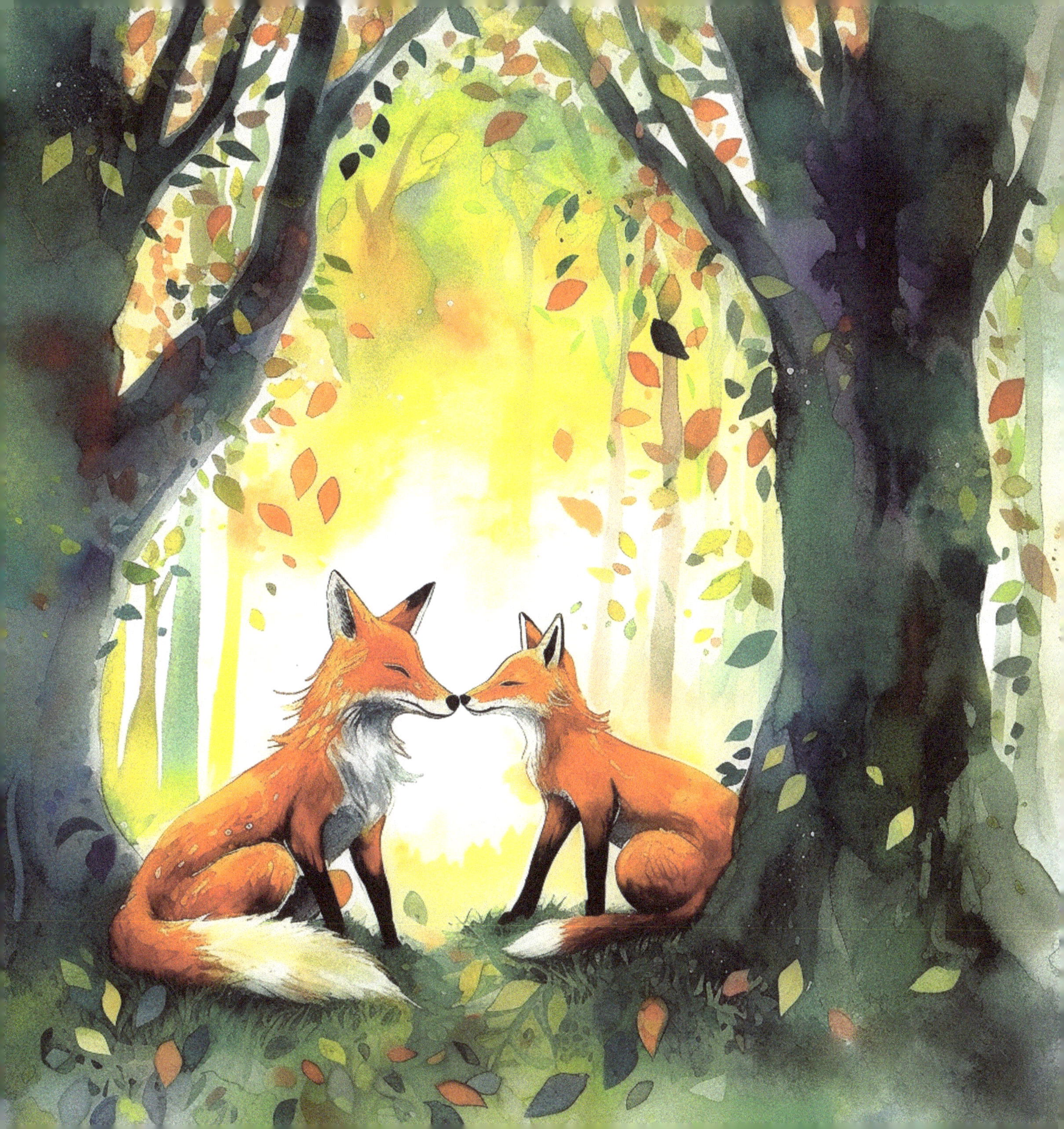

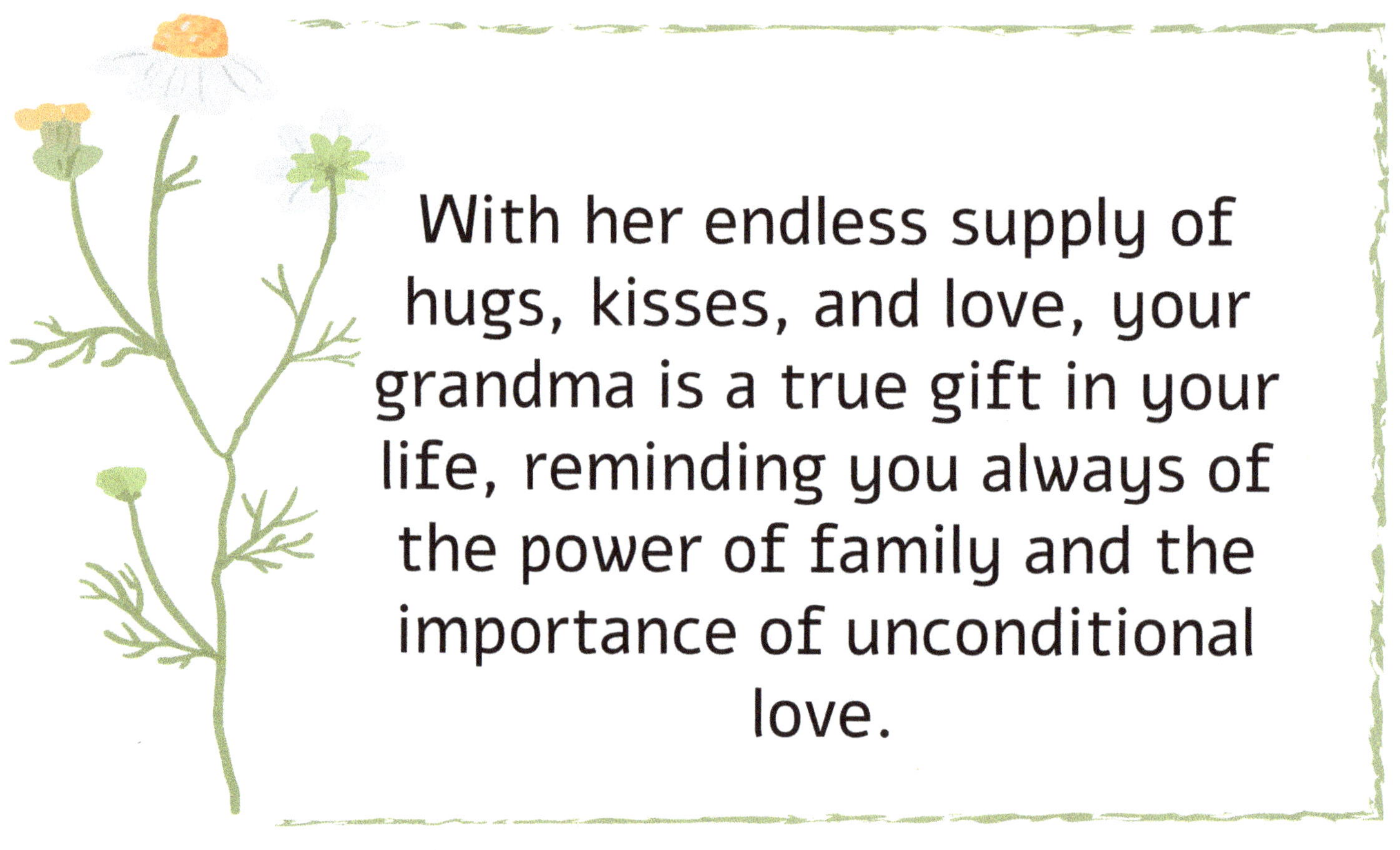

With her endless supply of hugs, kisses, and love, your grandma is a true gift in your life, reminding you always of the power of family and the importance of unconditional love.

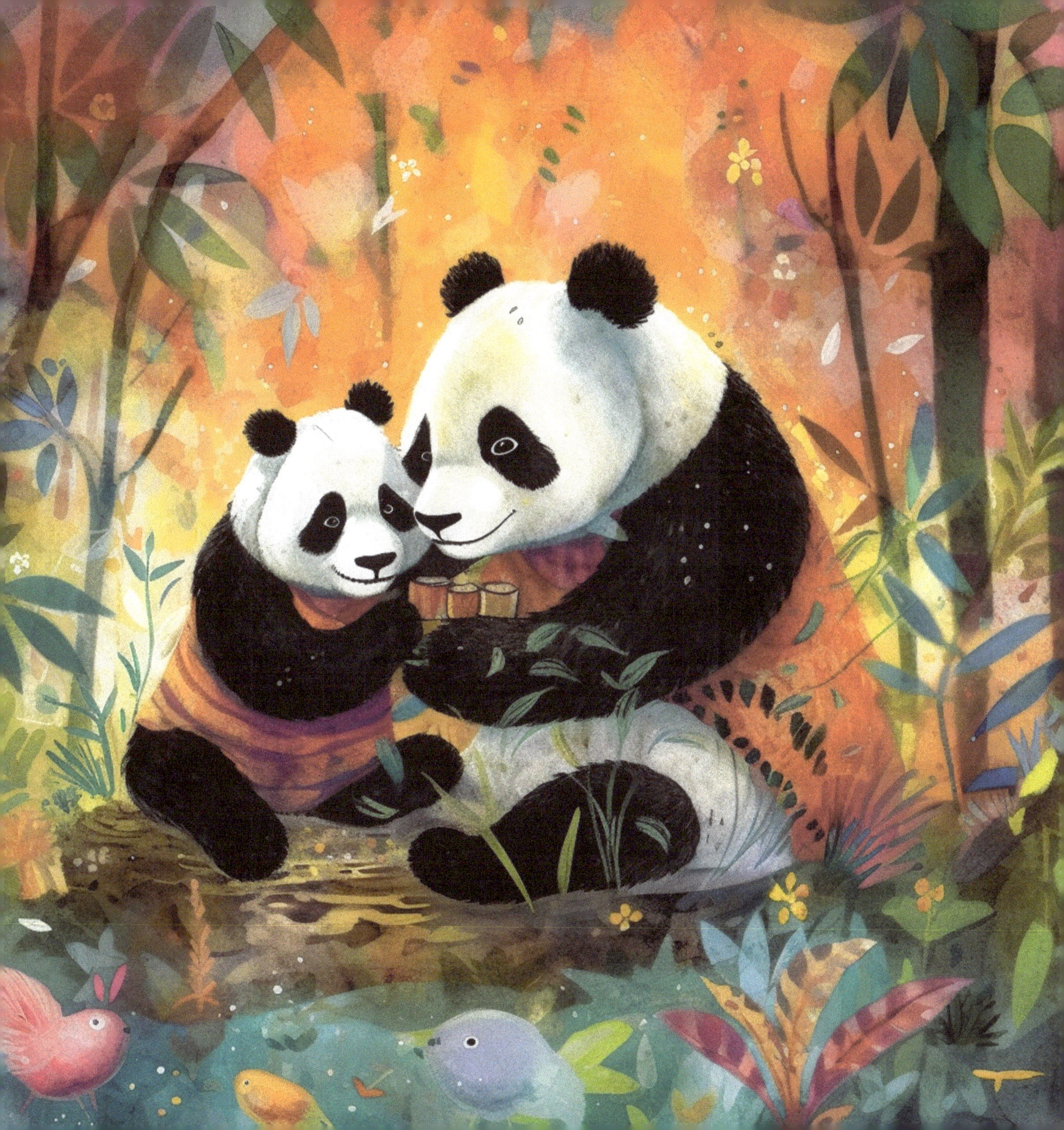

Your grandma is the secret keeper of family recipes and traditions, passing down her knowledge and expertise to create cherished memories that will last a lifetime.

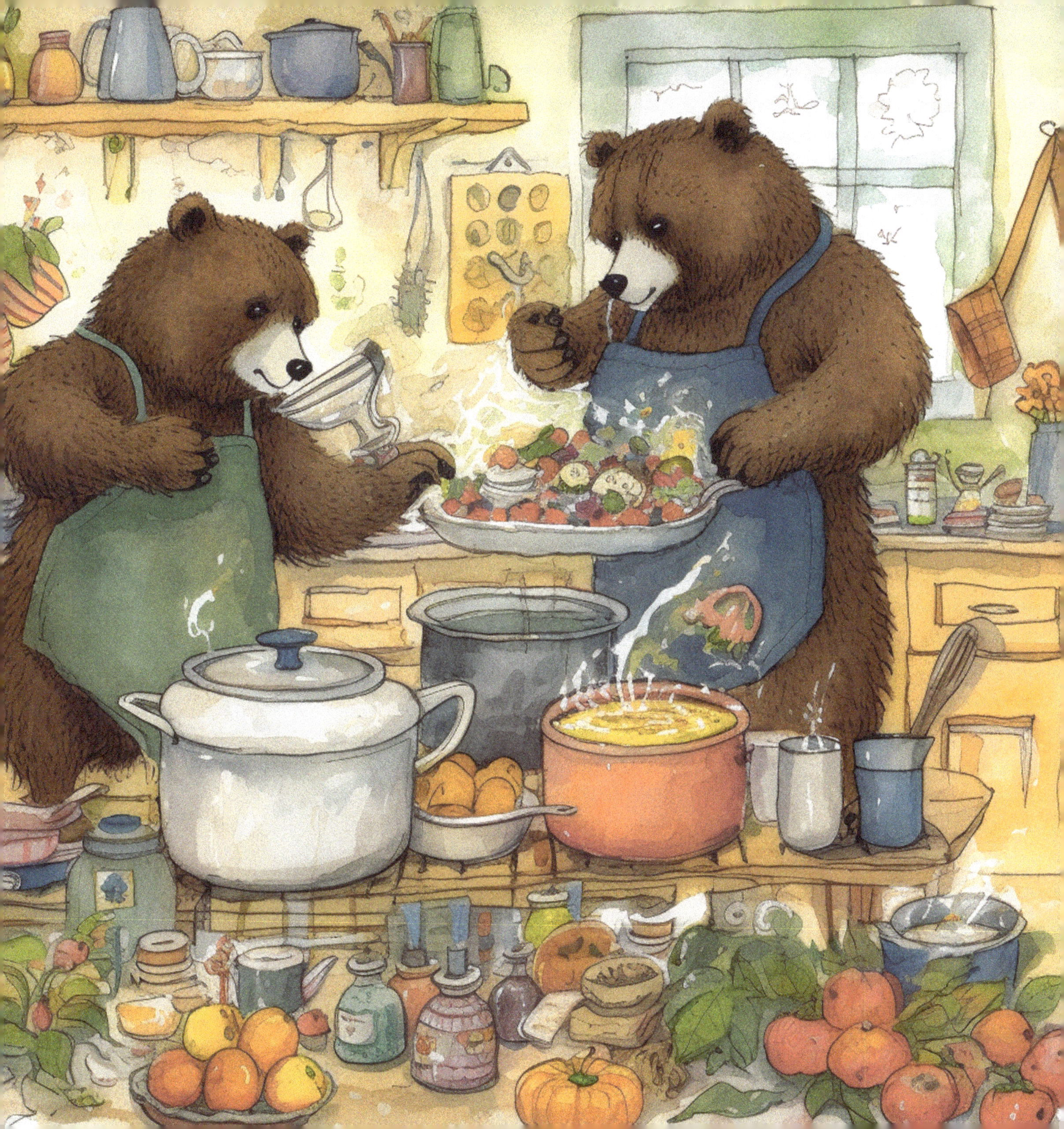

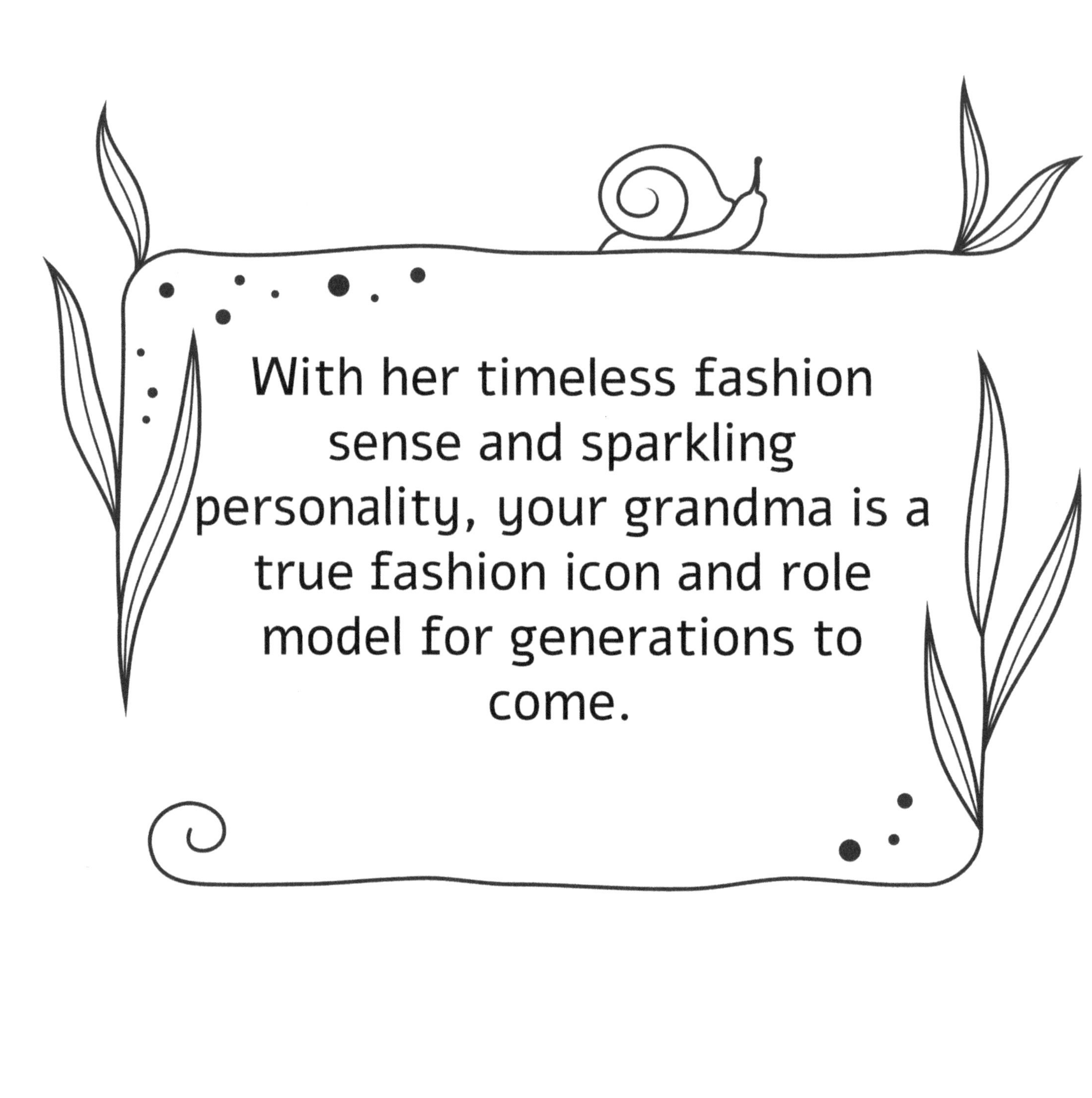

With her timeless fashion
sense and sparkling
personality, your grandma is a
true fashion icon and role
model for generations to
come.

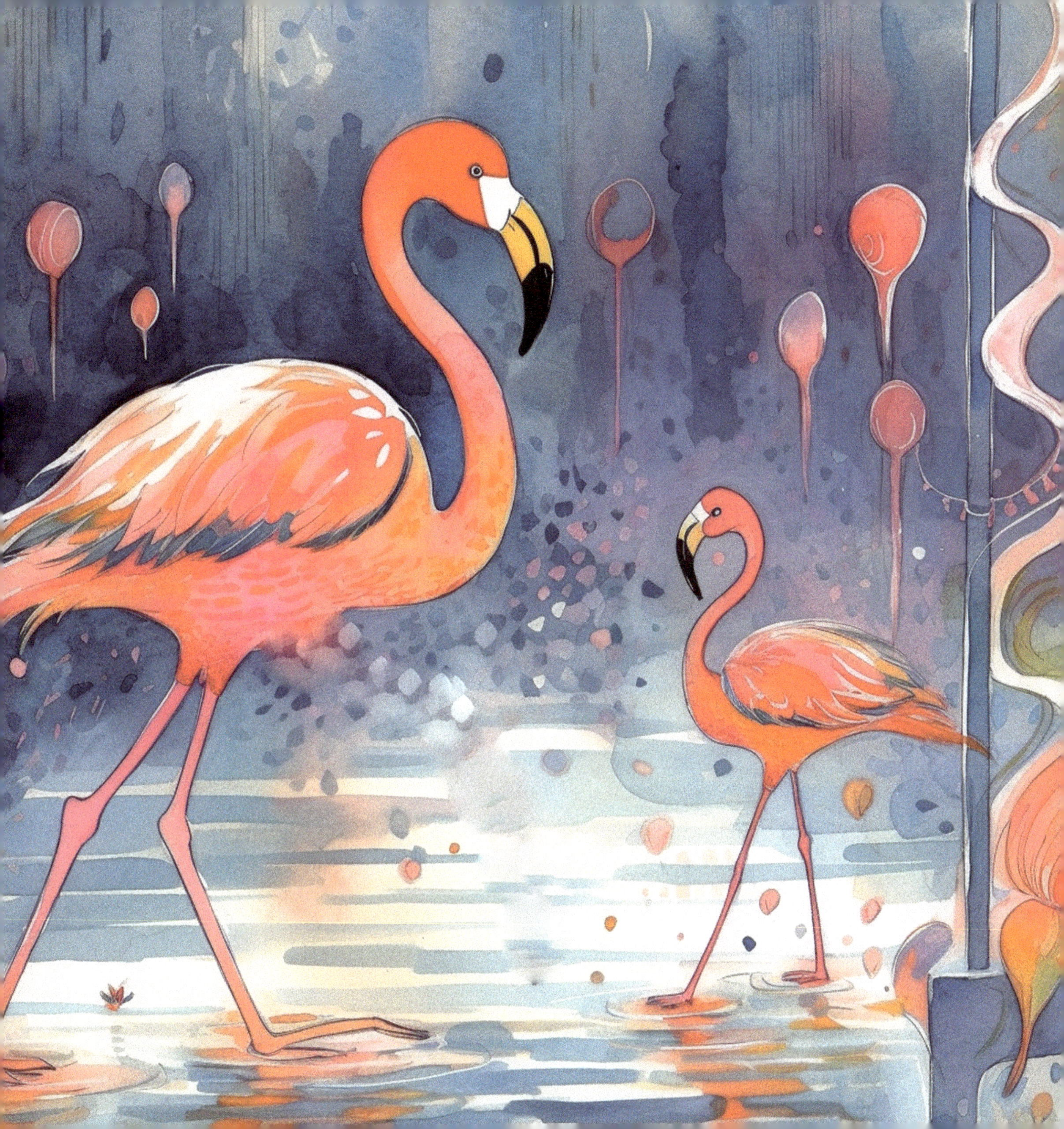

Your grandma is a true multitasker, juggling endless responsibilities with grace and poise, and always making time for you.

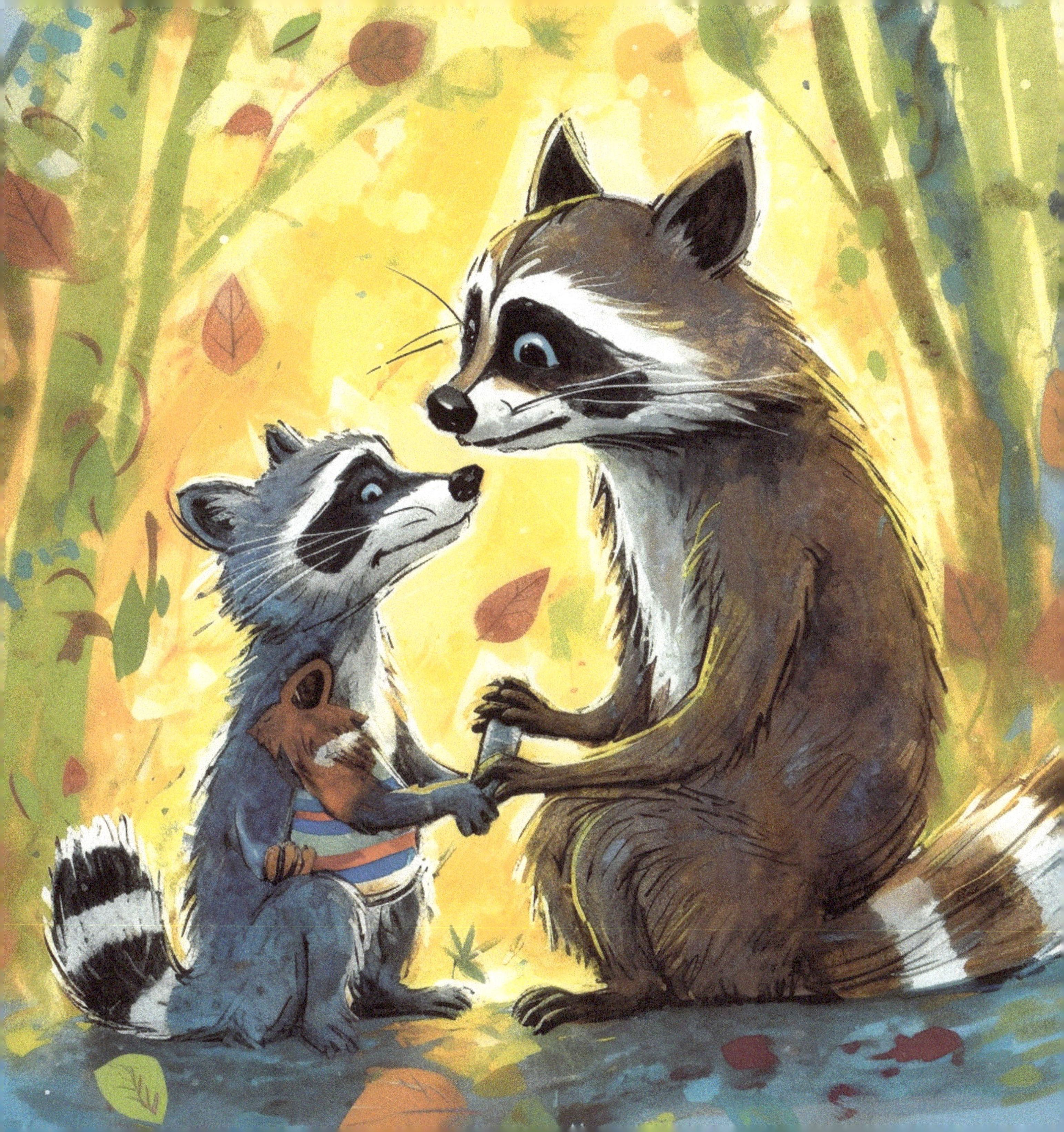

With her endless love, patience, and generosity, your grandma is a true gift in your life, and you feel so grateful and blessed to have her as a part of your family.

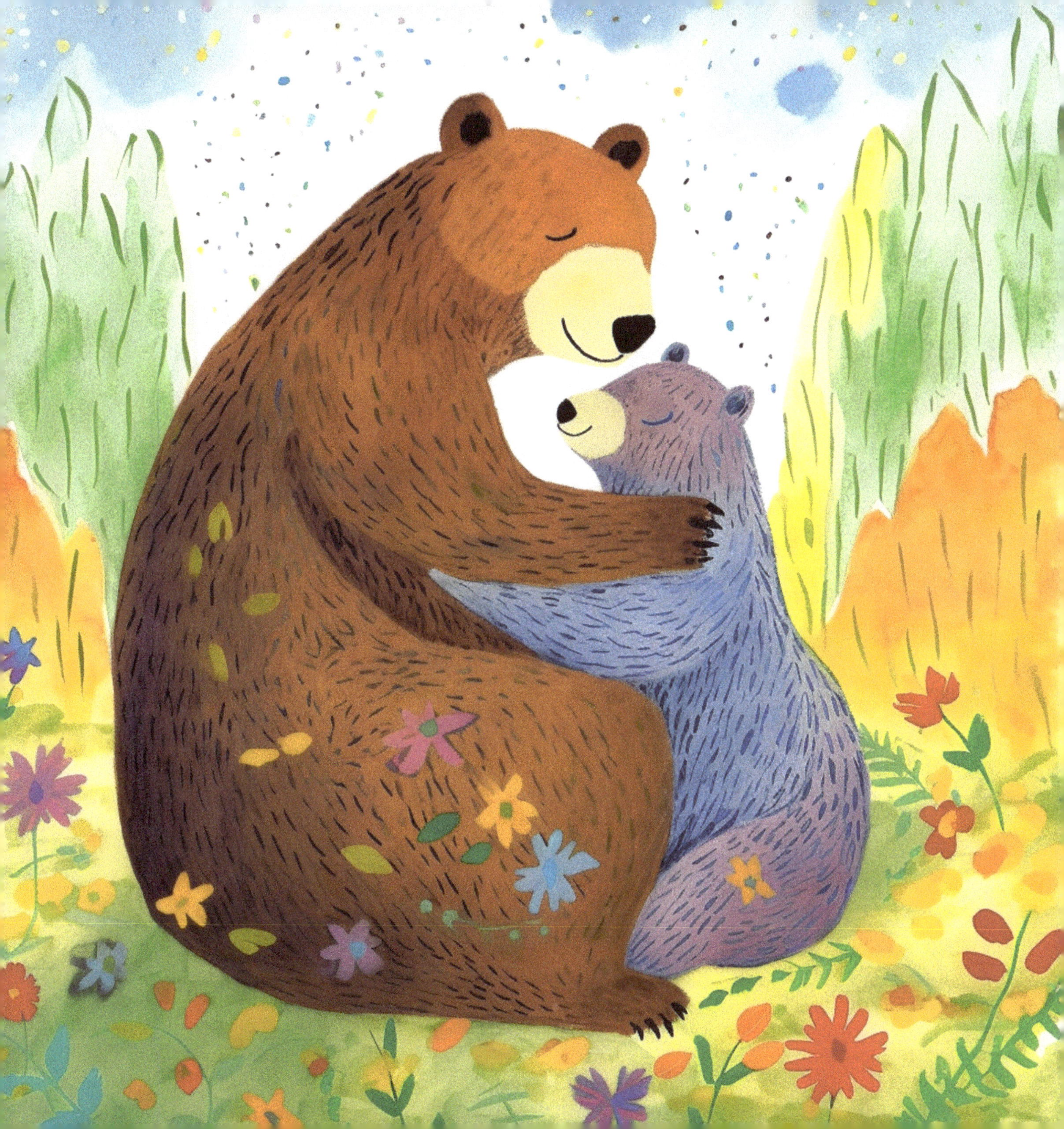

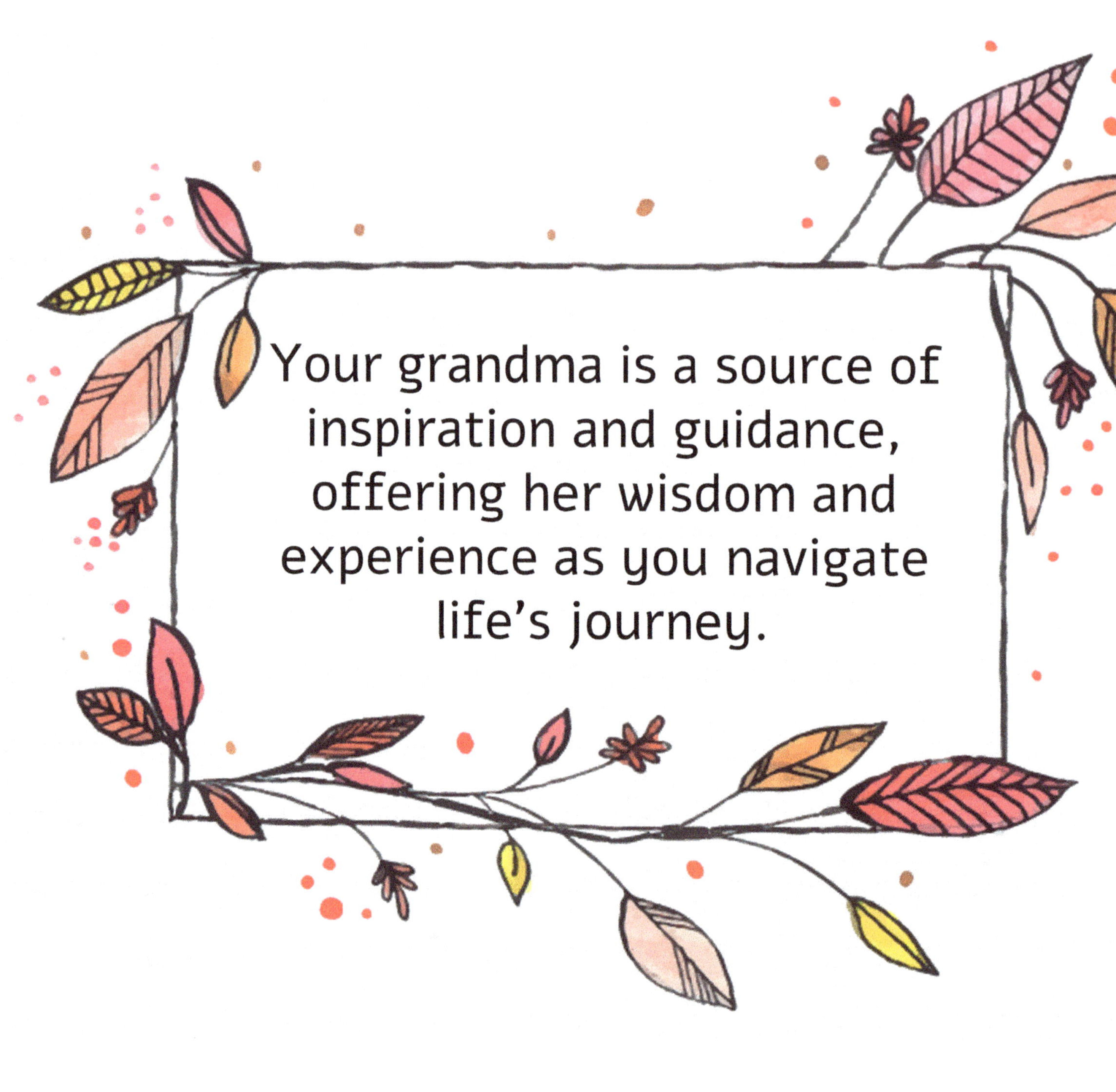

Your grandma is a source of
inspiration and guidance,
offering her wisdom and
experience as you navigate
life's journey.

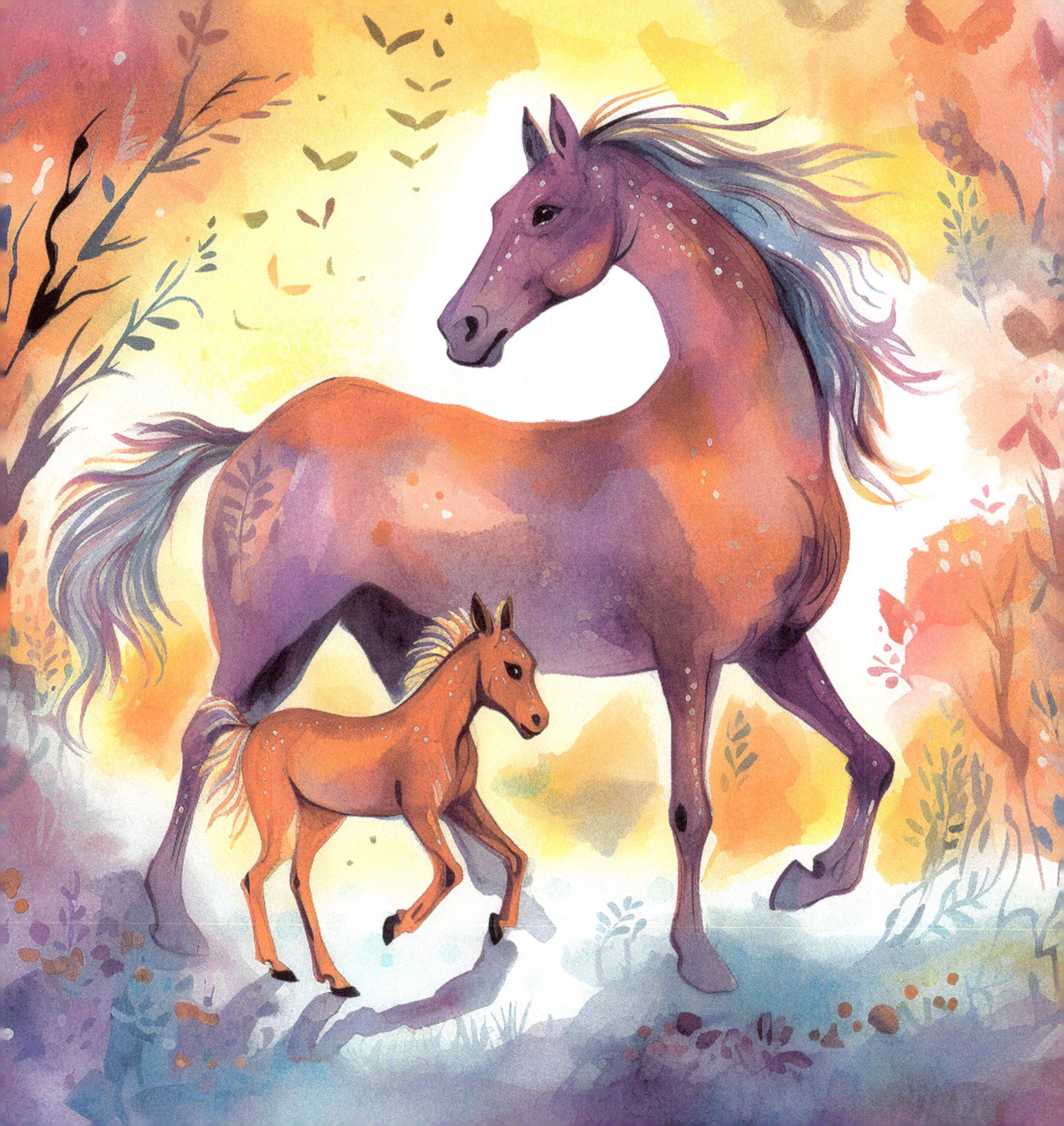

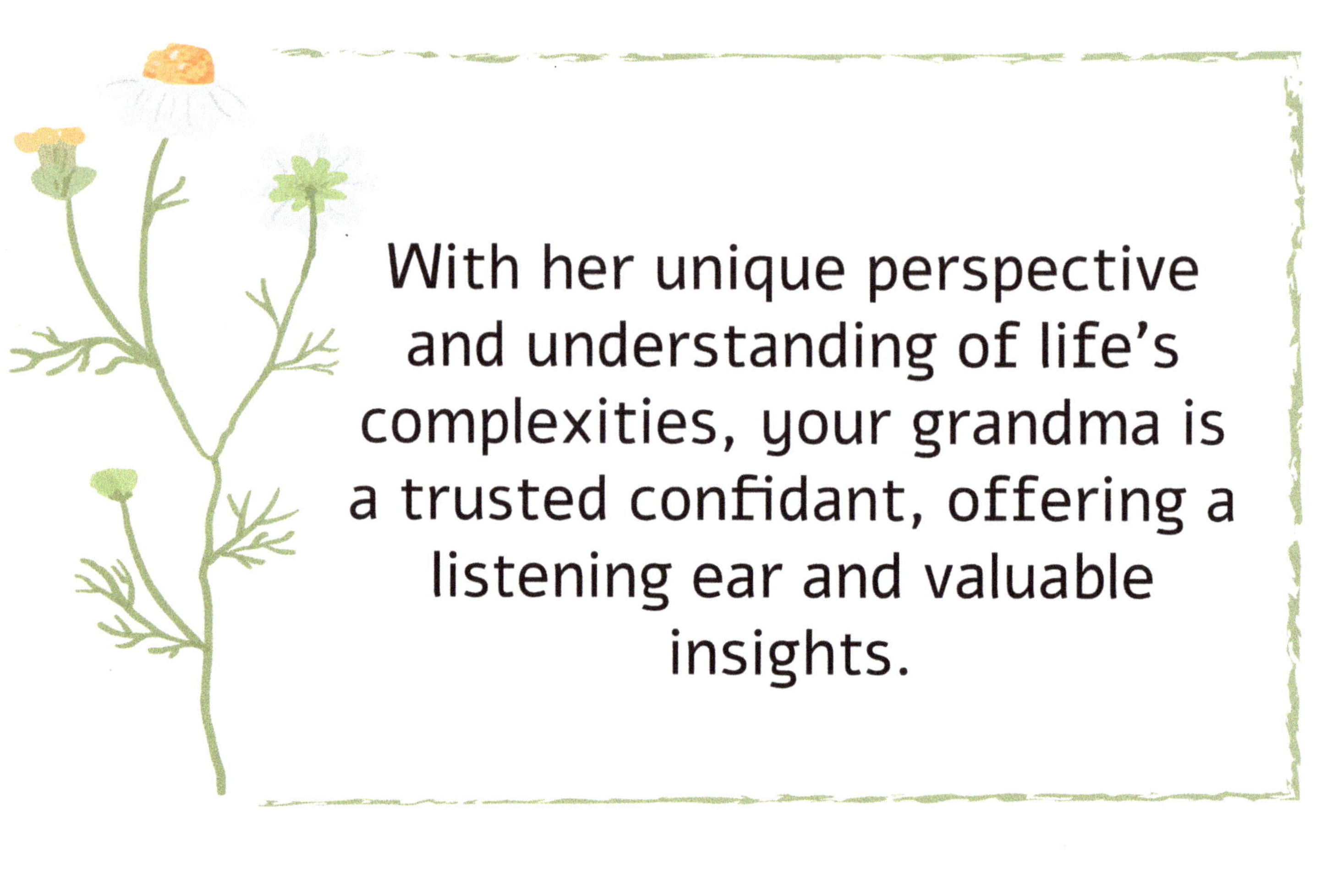

With her unique perspective and understanding of life's complexities, your grandma is a trusted confidant, offering a listening ear and valuable insights.

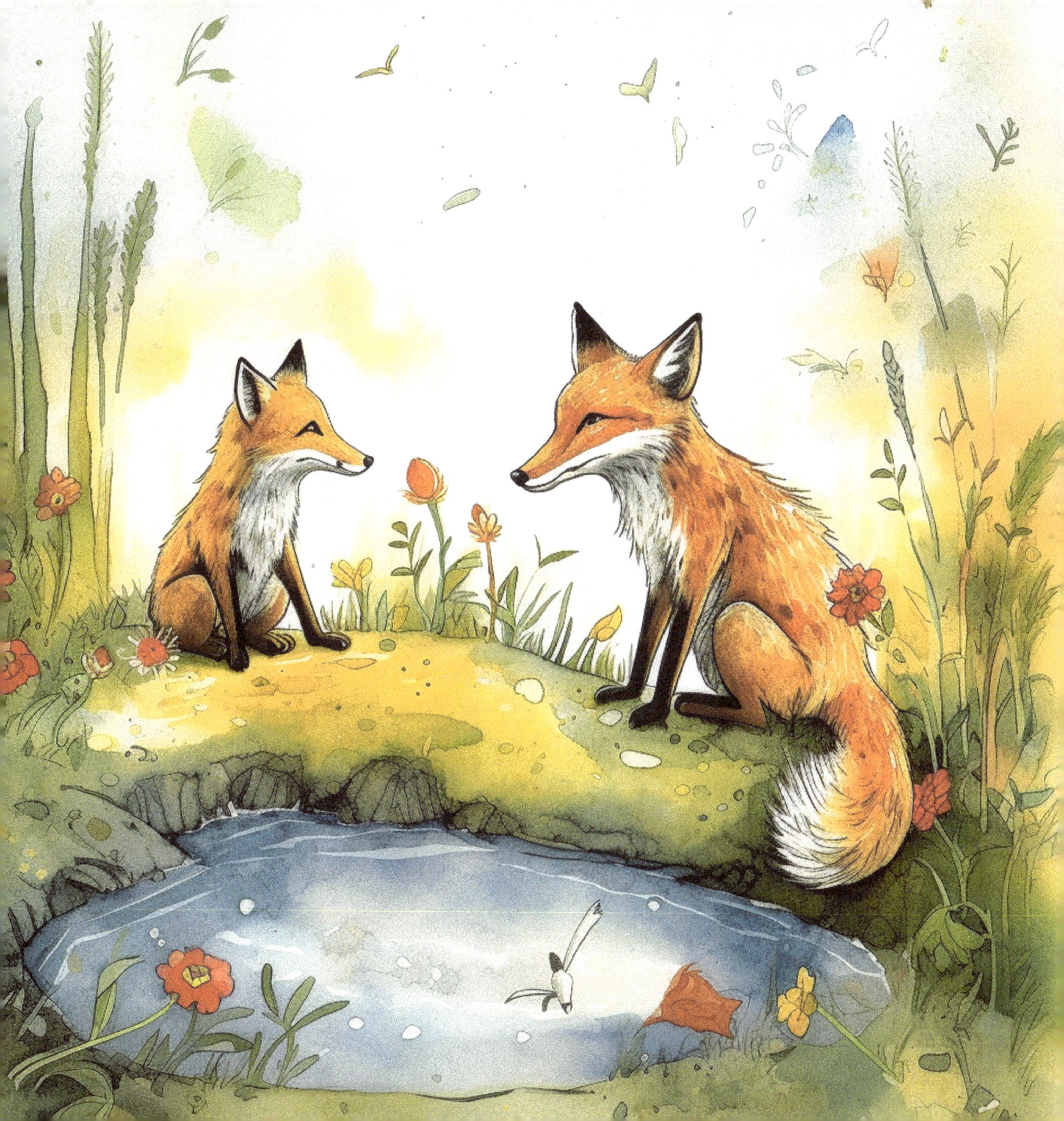

Your grandma is a true guardian angel, offering her love and support as you face life's challenges and uncertainties

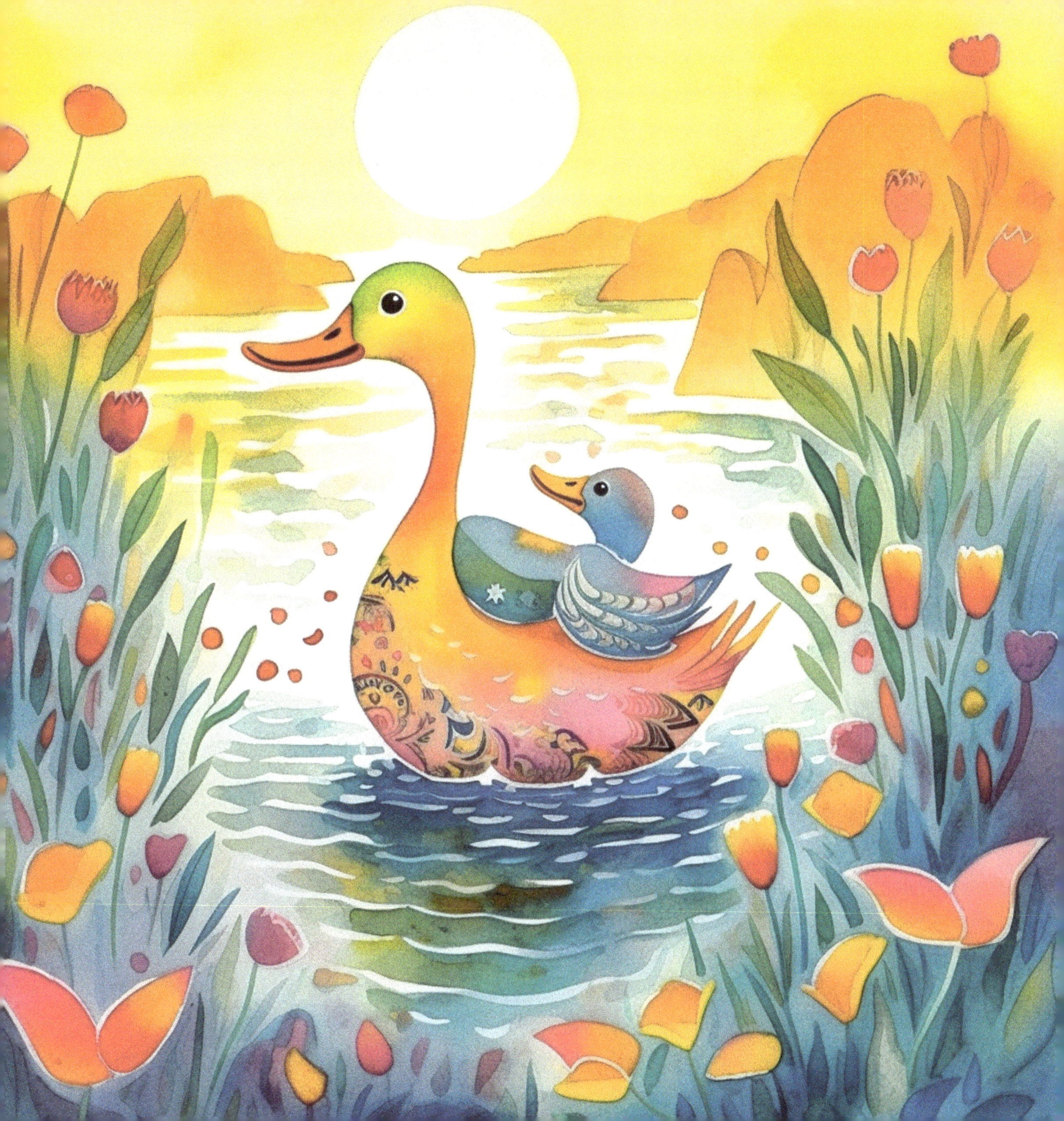

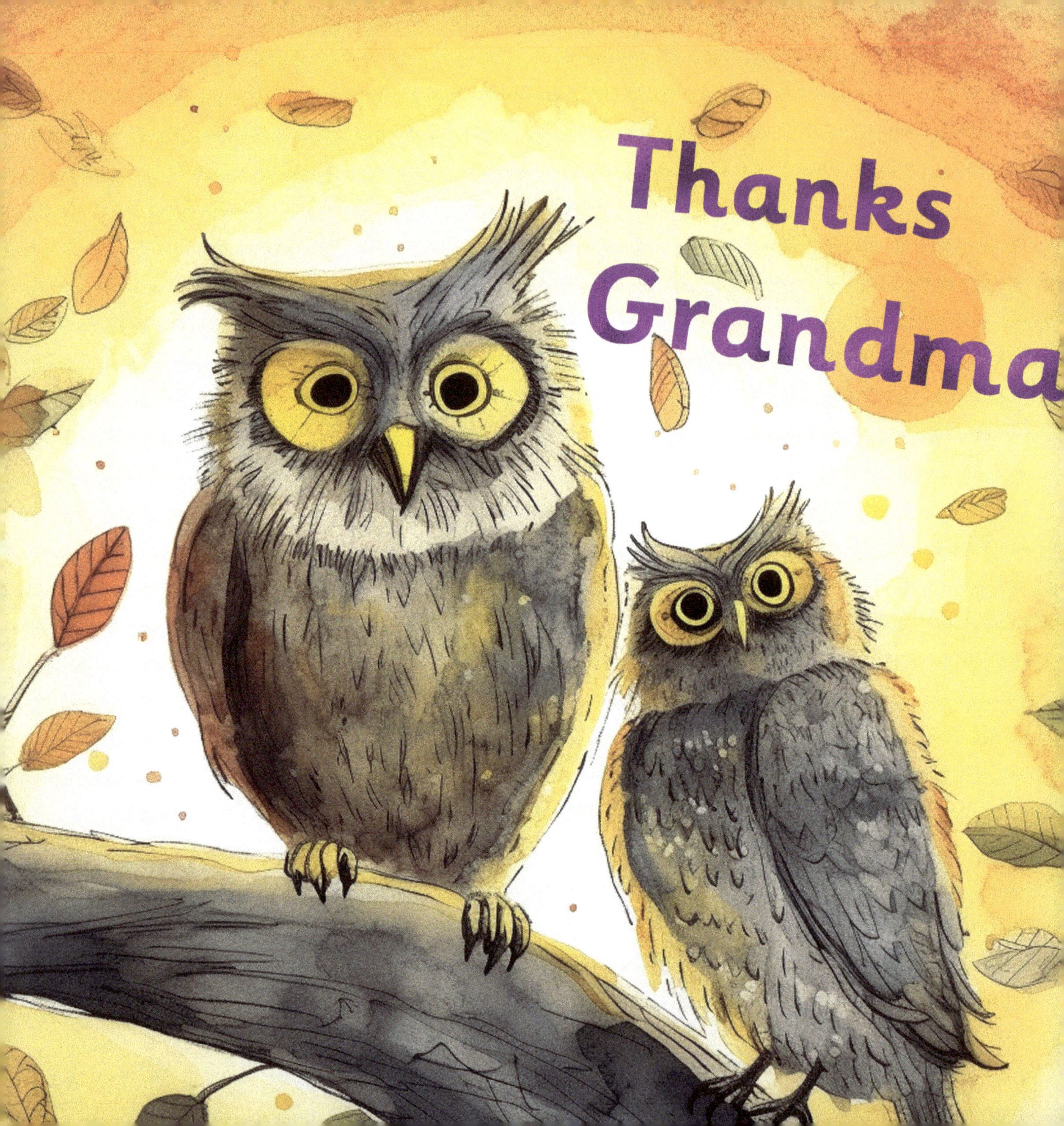
Thanks
Grandma